Understanding Waves *and* Wave Motion

RANDALL McPARTLAND

 Cavendish
Square

New York

Published in 2015 by Cavendish Square Publishing, LLC
243 5th Avenue, Suite 136, New York, NY 10016

CPSIA Compliance Information: Batch #WW15CSQ

All websites were available and accurate when this book was sent to press.

Library of Congress Cataloging-in-Publication Data

McPartland, Randall.
Understanding waves and wave motion / by Randall McPartland.
p. cm. — (Mastering physics)
Includes index.
ISBN 978-1-5026-0137-7 (hardcover) ISBN 978-1-5026-0134-6 (ebook)
1. Waves — Juvenile literature. 2. Wave-motion, Theory of — Juvenile literature. I. Title.
QC157.M337 2015
531.1133—d23

Editor: Fletcher Doyle
Senior Copy Editor: Wendy A. Reynolds
Art Director: Jeffrey Talbot
Senior Designer: Amy Greenan
Senior Production Manager: Jennifer Ryder-Talbot
Production Editor: David McNamara
Photo Research by J8 Media

The photographs in this book are used by permission and through the courtesy of: Cover photo and page 1, Shalom Jacobovitz/File:2010 mavericks competition.jpg/Wikimedia Commons; BarryTuck/Shutterstock.com, 4; sumnersgraphicsinc/iStock/Thinkstock, 6; Jan Mika/Shutterstock.com, 8; Francisco Leong/AFP/Getty Images, 11; Andrey_Popov/Shutterstock.com, 12; PictureInFocus/iStock/Thinkstock, 13; NASA/Photo Researchers/Getty Images, 14; photoiconix/Shutterstock.com, 16; File:Nernst, Einstein, Planck, Millikan, Laue in 1931.jpg/Wikimedia Commons, 17; Amy Greenan for Cavendish Square, 18–19; Brocken Inaglory/File:Diving grebe.jpg/Wikimedia Commons, 19; Library of Congress – Underwood and Underwood/Getty Images, 20; Designua/Shutterstock.com, 22; Bob Thomas Sports Photography/Getty Images, 24; MCT/Newscom, 25; U.S. Navy photo by Mass Communication Specialist 3rd Class Dugan Flynn/File:US Navy 111007-N-EZ913-085 Electrician's Mate 3rd Class Samuel Cabaruvias, from Compton, Calif., uses an oscilloscope to test an electric motor abo.jpg/Wikimedia Commons, 27; Michael Dunning/Photographer's Choice/Getty Images, 28; Amy Greenan for Cavendish Square, 30; Dorling Kindersley/Getty Images, 31; Designua/Shutterstock.com, 32; File:Doppler effect.svg/Wikimedia Commons, 33; katielittle/Shutterstock.com, 34; Stocktrek Images/Thinkstock, 36; John Fowler/File:Very Large Array, 2012.jpg/Wikimedia Commons, 38; AP Photo/Diane Claridge, 40; Kiyoshi Ota/Bloomberg/Getty Images, 42.

Printed in the United States of America

CONTENTS

INTRODUCTION

W hen most people hear the word "**waves**," they think of high tide at the oceans, with large, cresting waves breaking on the beach. However, whether you can see them or not, you are surrounded by waves. When you use your cellphone to call a friend, you are sending and receiving sound waves. When you heat pizza in your microwave, you are using waves named (you guessed it) microwaves to cook. Radio waves allow you to hear the latest music in your car. Although most waves are not visible to the naked eye, they are a huge part of modern life. Wave properties have also been part of the basic survival skills of some animals such as bats and whales, which use waves to navigate, in order to measure distances, to find food, and to locate other members of their species. Understanding the basic properties of waves helps us understand the world better.

In the sixteenth and seventeenth centuries, scientists began to develop their theories based on experiments and mathematical analyses rather than on the observation of natural events. This period in history is sometimes called the scientific revolution. During this time, scientists became fascinated with the study of waves, and saw them as a means of unlocking the secrets of Earth and even our universe. Thanks to physicists' understanding of waves, some amazing technologies have been invented, including sonar (sound navigation ranging), radio, television, cellular phones, and wireless Internet service.

The oceans provide one of the few examples of visible waves.

Seeing your favorite band perform your favorite song in concert and watching a music video of the song on the Internet are both possible because of sound waves, even if the two experiences are very different. The study of waves can be broken down into their two distinct categories—**electromagnetic waves** and **mechanical waves**. Understanding the difference between these two types of waves and how they interact with their **medium** (or don't interact) will increase understanding of the world in general.

Creating a large disturbance in ropes is a great form of exercise.

ONE
Understanding the Basics of Waves

You are almost always interacting with waves. While most waves are not visible to the eye, some are. When watching a wave at the beach, you can start to gain an understanding of how they act, including the almost rhythmic rise and fall of the waves. Watch long enough and you will start to see the patterns these waves follow, reaching a **crest** and then crashing down. Waves you cannot see follow patterns as well. Any sound you hear is reaching you through sound waves, and like ocean waves, they demonstrate specific behaviors. As you learn more about waves, you will discover that they can travel through any state of matter, including solid, liquid, or gas. You will also realize that waves can travel in any direction, including up and down, and left to right. Knowing this can help you understand how to recognize waves by their basic properties.

MAKING WAVES

A mechanical wave can best be described as a **disturbance** that **propagates**, or travels, through a medium from one point to another. There is a simple experiment you can do at home or in the

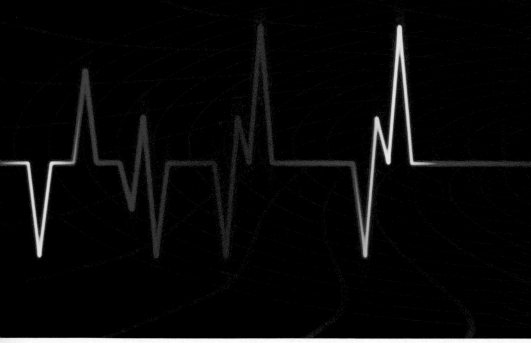

The straight lines between pulses are the equilibrium position.

classroom to simulate a wave by using a piece of rope or heavy string that is about 12 to 15 feet (about 4 meters to 5 meters) long. Tie one end of the rope or string to the back of a chair or to a doorknob, and hold the other end in your hand. Extend the rope or string as far as it will go and hold it out straight but with a little slack. When you hold it this way, there are no waves traveling through the rope. This is called an **equilibrium** position, or a rest position.

First, let's illustrate a pulse. Move the rope or string quickly with your hand once, up and then down. You will notice that the rope or string also moves up, down, and then returns to its original rest position. This is a pulse. A pulse is a single disturbance propagating through a medium from one point to another.

Now move the rope or string end in a large, quick repeated up-and-down motion. By moving it this way with your hand, you're creating a periodic disturbance in the equilibrium position. You will notice a continuous motion of alternating hills and valleys that appear to move through the rope. You have now created a true wave. Unlike a pulse, a continuous wave is a periodic, or repeating, disturbance that travels through a medium from one point to another.

Understanding Waves and Wave Motion

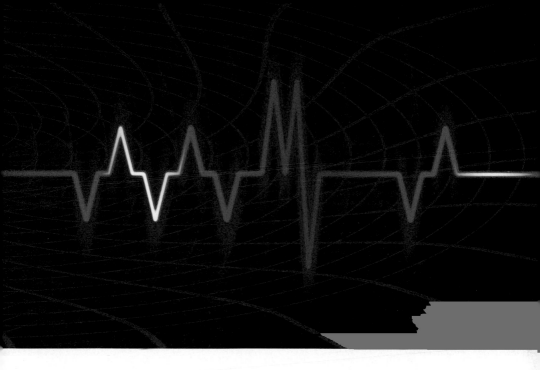

MOVING THROUGH THE MEDIUM

Artistic media are the materials that artists use to create paintings, sculptures, or photographs. For example, Paul Gauguin expressed himself through the artistic medium of painting, whereas Ansel Adams communicated his ideas through the medium of photography. A medium is a substance or a material through which something is transported from its source to another location. Imagine that you are in an art class and you want to create a likeness of an apple. You may choose to draw the apple with a pencil, or to sculpt it from clay. In this case, the media are the pencil and the clay. Until your idea of how an apple should look travels through a medium (the pencil or the clay), it cannot be communicated. The same is true for many types of waves. A wave in the ocean travels through the medium of water. When your science teacher gives a lecture on physics, the sound of his or her voice travels through the medium of air.

Big Wave Surfing

S urfers are always tracking waves, looking for the largest waves to ride to the shore. In late 2013, a Brazilian surfer by the name of Carlos Burle amazed onlookers and may have set a world record in Portugal when he rode a wave estimated to be 100 feet (30 m) tall. Burle, a well-known big wave surfer, was riding the waves off the coast of Nazare, Portugal, a location known for record-breaking waves. The previous record for big wave surfing had been a 78-foot (24 m) wave caught by Garrett McNamara in 2011. McNamara had also caught his big wave in Nazare, which has become the hotspot for big wave surfers. In fact, the size of the waves inspired McNamara to call the area "the eighth wonder of the world."

Nazare's unique geography allows for the creation of such large waves. Generally, as a wave approaches the shore, the ocean floor slows the speed and reduces the size of the wave. However, Nazare has a 16,000-foot deep (4,877 m) canyon approaching its shore, which can magnify large ocean waves that get created by winter Atlantic storms. To get an idea of the canyon's depth, it is more than two-and-a-half times deeper than the Grand Canyon, which is only 6,000 feet deep (1,829 m). This geographical anomaly is not limited to Nazare. Similar undersea canyons also exist near Hawaii, California, and Tahiti.

Carlos Burle rides his record wave off the coast of Portugal.

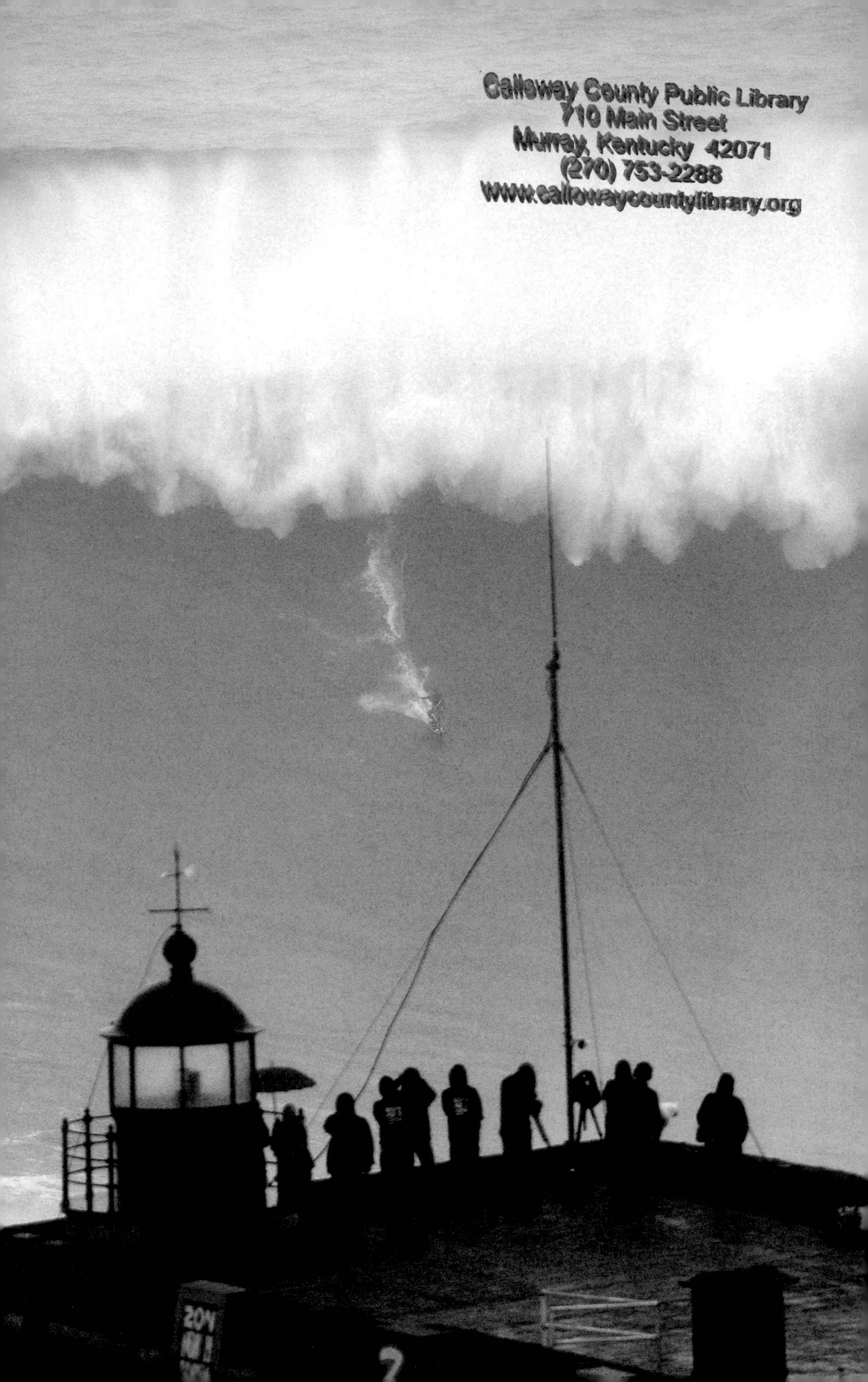

A line of dominoes does not return to its original state after a disturbance.

THE ENERGY OF WAVES

How does a wave maintain the energy to travel through the rope? How does it manage to move from the tips of your fingers to the doorknob? When understanding the propagation of waves, it is important to think of the medium as being interconnected particles, or parts that can interact with each other. Energy is sent from the source of a disturbance from one particle to its neighboring particle. Imagine a set of dominoes lined up next to one another on a table. When you tap the first domino, the force or energy that is sent from your finger to the first domino will transfer to the second domino, and so on. When you tap a domino, you are transporting energy by displacing or moving the medium (the dominoes). However, when a wave transports a disturbance, it does so without displacing matter. After being tapped, the dominoes fall down. They do not return to their original upright position. When a wave passes through a medium, the medium always returns to its original rest position.

Understanding Waves and Wave Motion

The ocean always returns to its original depth after a cresting wave passes through it.

This is called **elasticity.** Its effect is similar to the way in which a stretched-out rubber band can return to its original shape. Elasticity is sometimes referred to as an energy transport phenomenon. The fact that a wave can travel through a medium without permanently displacing matter is another defining characteristic of a wave. It is one way in which we can identify a wave.

The rope experiment can also effectively demonstrate how energy transport occurs. As you move the rope to initialize the wave, the energy moves along the rope, causing the next part of the rope to move and the previous part of the rope to return to its original position. This process continues along the rope until it reaches the end point, and then it starts heading back along the rope. Its continual movement means that as the wave arcs up, it doesn't remain in that position—it eventually works its way back down again. Just as when a wave moves through the ocean, the water eventually returns to its original depth. In all situations, the changes that occur to a medium (water, air, and so on) are only temporary. The wave moves through the medium, resulting in a short-term change to the medium.

Understanding the Basics of Waves

Mechanical waves need a
medium—they cannot pass
through the vacuum of space.

TWO

Understanding the Types of Waves

S tudying the basics of waves can give you an understanding of all waves, as waves share a number of characteristics. However, to truly learn about waves, you also need to consider the way categories of waves are different. Some of the differences are readily apparent. A mechanical wave, like a sound wave, needs a medium to travel through. On the other hand, electromagnetic waves, like your pizza-heating microwaves, do not need a medium for travel.

TWO TYPES OF WAVES

You now know that determining whether or not a wave requires a medium is the first step in categorizing it. Electromagnetic waves can propagate through a vacuum (empty space). Some examples of electromagnetic waves are radio waves, microwaves, X rays, and light waves. We generally divide the electromagnetic range of waves into radio waves and light waves. The propagation of electromagnetic waves is also referred to as electromagnetic radiation.

Mechanical waves cannot travel through a vacuum. If you were to stand on the moon and play a song on a violin, you would not hear the sound because you are standing in a vacuum. There is no air (or medium) on the moon for the sound to travel through. However, you would be able to see the light from the sun, because a light wave is able to transmit energy through empty space.

There are ways to categorize a wave even further. The next characteristic examines how a wave travels.

The direction of movement of mechanical waves is based on the elastic movement of the medium through which they are propagated. There are three main categories in which a mechanical wave can be classified: **transverse** waves, **longitudinal** waves, and surface waves.

Transverse Wave

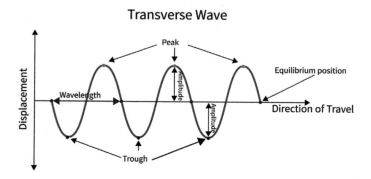

Longitudinal Wave

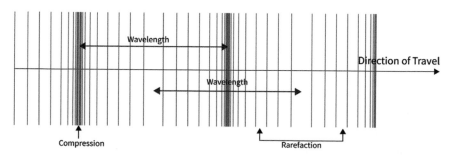

Mechanical waves are defined by the direction of their particles in relation to the direction of the waves.

Nobel Prize winners Walther Nernst, Albert Einstein, Max Planck, R.A. Millikan, and Max von Laue in 1931.

Defining Light

The nature of light had been debated since the time of the ancient Greeks. Many Greek scientists argued that light emitted from sources as a stream of particles, while Aristotle postulated that light moved in a wave, similar to those in the ocean. The debate continued into the seventeenth century, with rival physicists arguing whether light is a particle or a wave.

English physicist Sir Isaac Newton (1642–1727) was the first to declare that light was a particle, or made up of tiny molecules of matter. This idea was called the corpuscular theory of light. Christian Huygens (1629–1695), a Dutch physicist, argued that light traveled in waves and discounted Newton's theories. Experiments seemed to validate Huygens' wave theory, and James Maxwell defined four equations that demonstrate that light behaved like electromagnetic waves.

In 1900, German physicist Max Planck (1858–1947) introduced wave-particle duality (quantum theory), which stated that light waves behave as both waves and particles. Einstein used this theory to explain the photoelectric effect, which had long baffled physicists. Further research and experiments by other physicists, including Arthur Compton and Louis-Victor de Broglie, strengthened this theory that light has properties of both particles and waves. However, the debate is still not settled to everyone's satisfaction. As a result, there are still some alternative theories about the nature of light.

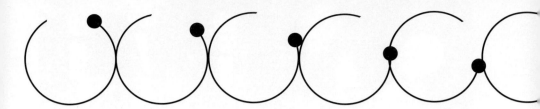

If the particles of a medium move in a direction perpendicular to the direction in which the wave moves, the wave is transverse. Our experiment with the rope is an excellent example of a transverse wave. The wave you created was moving in a horizontal direction. It transferred energy from your hand to the doorknob. Meanwhile, the rope (medium) moved in a vertical direction. It temporarily displaced itself upward and downward in the shape of hills and valleys.

The important thing to remember about a transverse wave is that the disturbing or actuating force is perpendicular to the direction of the wave. Transverse waves can be either mechanical or electromagnetic.

In a longitudinal wave, the particles of a medium move in a direction parallel to the direction in which the wave moves. Suppose a vibration is sent from a source to a particle in a medium. If it is a longitudinal wave, the particle will push its energy onto the neighboring particle. The particles of the medium are temporarily displaced from left to right in a horizontal direction while the wave is also moving left to right in a horizontal direction.

A sound wave is an example of a longitudinal wave. Imagine that a friend across a room says, "Hello!" The sound makes its way across the room in a horizontal direction toward your ears. While the sound is traveling, it pushes air molecules against one another in a horizontal direction. Unlike the transverse wave, it doesn't move in the shape of hills and valleys. Instead, the sound wave moves in a repeating formation of **compressions** and **rarefactions**. Compressions are places in the medium that are pushed close together. Rarefactions are places in the medium that are spread apart.

Understanding Waves and Wave Motion

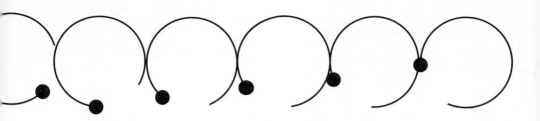

A diving Grebe creates a surface wave.

The third type of wave is a surface wave. This category of wave is what you see in the ocean. A surface wave will travel in a circular motion, moving up and down like a transverse wave, and heading toward shore like a longitudinal wave. Waves in the deeper part of the ocean only move parallel to the ocean floor, so these deeper waves are longitudinal waves.

Telephone inventor Alexander Graham Bell developed a way to measure sound levels as part of his work with the hearing impaired.

THREE

Breaking Down Waves

Transverse waves, which run perpendicular in their medium, hit high points and low points in their motion. The high points, like the top of a mountain, are called crests, while their low points, similar to valleys, are known as **troughs**. A wave reaches its crest when it will not have any further upward displacement, and its trough is the point on the wave when it has reached is maximum downward displacement. Both of these values are measured against the original rest position of the wave.

The crests and troughs represent the presence of a disturbance in a medium. Earlier, we learned that when a rope is held out straight in a rest position, there are no waves present in the rope. Once your hand moved the rope up and down, you noticed that a disturbance was sent through the length of rope. How do we measure this disturbance that is moving through the rope? If you move the rope by making short up-and-down motions with your hand, the crests and troughs in the rope are smaller. However, if you move the rope by making long up-and-down motions with your hand, the crests and troughs in the rope are larger. To measure the

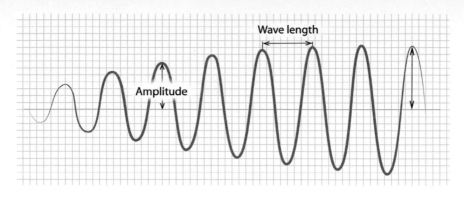

The amplitude of a sound wave increases when the size of the disturbance grows.

level of a disturbance in a transverse wave, we measure the height of the crest (or the depth of the trough) from the rest position. This distance is known as the **amplitude** of a wave. The amplitude is one way of measuring a wave.

HOW HIGH, HOW OFTEN

To determine a wave's amplitude, the maximum distance the wave moves from its equilibrium or rest position must be measured. The **wavelength** (or length of one complete wave cycle) of a transverse wave is the distance from one crest to the next crest or from one trough to the next trough. The wavelength is sometimes represented by the Greek symbol λ (lambda).

So how do we measure the amplitude of a longitudinal wave, which has compressions and rarefactions rather than crests and troughs? In a longitudinal wave (for example, a sound wave), the amplitude is the maximum distance a particle is pushed (due to compression) or pulled (due to rarefaction) from its equilibrium position. This is usually measured as the amount of deviation of pressure above and below atmospheric pressure. A unit of pressure is called a pascal. There are different types of instruments that are used to measure pressure. An example of an instrument that measures air pressure is a barometer. It can measure slight changes in atmospheric pressure that indicate changes in weather.

Scottish-born American scientist Alexander Graham Bell (1847–1922) is best known for inventing the telephone, but he also worked with people who were deaf or who had hearing impairments. His wife Mabel was deaf, and his mother, who became an accomplished pianist despite the fact she suffered the total loss of her hearing, was also a major influence on his work. He developed a system for measuring loudness that enabled him to easily determine the range of a person's hearing. The unit of measurement in this system was named for him and called a bel. A decibel is equal to one-tenth of a bel, and is denoted as "dB." A reference sound level corresponding to a pressure of 20 micropascals (20×10^{-6} Pa) is designated as 0 dB. (This intensity in energy flow per unit area is the value 1×10^{-12} watts/m^2.) This is a sound level that a person with normal hearing can just barely hear. A sound level that is ten times louder than this reference sound level is 10 dB. A sound level that is 100 times as loud as the reference sound level is 20 dB, and something 1,000 times as loud as the reference sound level is 30 dB. (The decibel scale measures sound intensity. It is logarithmic, so each increase of 10 dB means that the sound is ten times more intense or louder.)

When you measure a wave's amplitude, you are measuring the level of disturbance in a medium. If you gently tug on the rope in your experiment, the disturbance is low. If you forcefully yank on the rope, the disturbance will be high. The **magnitude** (the height or depth) of a disturbance is directly related to the level of force that is used to introduce that disturbance. For example, if you whisper a secret to your classmate during class, the initial force of disturbance in the sound wave is low. However, if you are blowing through a vuvuzela horn to support your favorite team, the disturbance that is traveling through the medium, the air in this case, is high.

Whenever you measure the amplitude of a mechanical wave, you are usually measuring its displacement in units of length (that is, in inches, feet, meters, etc.), or in pressure (in pascals or decibels).

The vuvuzela made the 2010 World Cup in South Africa a noisy affair.

The displacement can be transversal (perpendicular to the direction of wave travel), or longitudinal (in the direction of wave travel).

Electromagnetic waves do not require a medium to propagate. Therefore, when measuring the amplitude of an electromagnetic wave, we measure its electric field or the strength of its radiation. For light waves, which are electromagnetic waves, the amplitude can be linked to light intensity. For example, the intensity of light from a common light bulb is measured in units of lumens. The amplitude of radio waves can be related to radiated power. The strength of a radio station near its transmission tower is measured in kilowatts, or units of 1,000 watts. However, when the radio waves reach a radio, they are greatly weakened and are on the order of milliwatts, or units of one one-thousandth of a watt.

REPEATING A WAVE

To measure wavelength, we measure the distance of one repetition in a wave cycle. Similar to wavelength, a period is a measurement of the time that it takes to complete one wave cycle. To measure how often a cycle occurs in a wave, we measure the wave's **frequency**. If a cycle is repeated many times in a time interval, such as a second, the wave has a high frequency. If a cycle does not have

Tuning Out

Sound bites

Sound between 85 and 90 decibels can cause discomfort, and above 120 it can cause hearing damage:

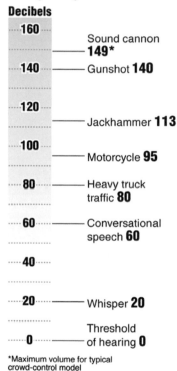

Decibels

Decibels	
160	
	Sound cannon **149***
140	Gunshot **140**
120	
	Jackhammer **113**
100	
	Motorcycle **95**
80	Heavy truck traffic **80**
60	Conversational speech **60**
40	
20	Whisper **20**
0	Threshold of hearing **0**

*Maximum volume for typical crowd-control model

When people fail to speak out against things that are wrong, or in defense of accusations made against them, we say their silence is deafening. This is, of course, physically impossible; silence can never make us deaf. The opposite is true, however. Loud noises can rob us of our hearing instantly or slowly, over time. As many as 16 percent of teens report hearing loss due to loud noise.

Very loud noises or impulse sounds, such as a bomb going off, can rupture your eardrums or damage the bones in your middle ear that pass along sound vibrations. More common is noise induced hearing loss (NIHL). This occurs when the ear is exposed to loud sounds over a period of time. Long, repeated exposure to sounds at 85 decibels and above can cause sensory hair cells within our ears to die, and they never grow back.

A live concert can leave us with tinnitus—a ringing in the ears that may or may not subside. Researchers also caution that people should monitor the volume of the music they are listening to through earphones. It is estimated that someone could safely listen to an mp3 player for 4.6 hours at 70 percent of full volume using the supplied earphones. However, listening at full volume for only five minutes a day could cause hearing loss.

many repetitions, it has a low frequency. Imagine the rope and the doorknob experiment again. Suppose it took exactly one second for the wave to travel from your hand to the doorknob. The number of crests (or troughs) that occur in one second represents the wave's frequency, or cycles per second. For example, AM radio waves have a low frequency, whereas microwaves operate at a higher frequency. Sound waves can also have a wide range of frequencies. Bats and dogs can detect high-frequency sound waves, whereas the human ear can detect only lower-frequency sound waves.

USING HERTZ TO MEASURE FREQUENCY

The unit of frequency, or one cycle per second, is commonly referred to as one hertz (1 Hz). The hertz is named for the German physicist Heinrich Rudolf Hertz (1857–1894), who, in the 1880s, was the first to transmit and receive radio waves. Radio waves are a form of electromagnetic wave. They do not require a medium to propagate. Hertz based his experiments on the theories of Scottish physicist James Clerk Maxwell (1831–1879), who postulated mathematical relationships between electricity and magnetism, thus founding the science of electromagnetics. Hertz used these findings to prove that the speed of radio waves in a vacuum is equal to the speed of light. The speed of light in a vacuum is 299,792,458 meters per second, or approximately 186,282 miles per second. If an object could travel at the speed of light it could circle Earth at the equator seven times in one second. He also demonstrated how magnetic and electric fields could detach themselves from a medium and travel through a vacuum. He called these new waves hertzian waves.

Although Hertz was the first to transmit and receive radio waves, messages weren't sent across radio waves until 1901, when a young Italian scientist, Guglielmo Marconi (1874–1937), read about Hertz's waves and became astounded by them. He wanted to find a way to send messages through them. In 1901, Marconi publicly announced that he had sent a radio signal in Morse code across the Atlantic Ocean from Cornwall, England, that was received in Newfoundland, Canada.

An oscilloscope measures fast-changing and repeating oscillations such as radio and sound waves. They have been used in sonar and radar on naval vessels.

Radio waves are a form of electromagnetic radiation (an electromagnetic wave). They behave in ways that are similar to those for light, X rays, gamma rays, and microwaves. However, to differentiate the types of electromagnetic waves, scientists have categorized them according to their frequencies, wavelengths, and energy. The waves are then classified into what is known as the electromagnetic spectrum.

In order to place a type of electromagnetic wave on the spectrum, scientists must measure the frequency of the wave. To do this, scientists track the time between two peaks in the electrical field. A single cycle per second is known as one hertz, so the total number of peaks that occur every second are the number of hertz. If a radio wave travels 2,000 periods in a second, it has a wavelength of 2 kHz (2 kilohertz). This is a low radio frequency, and in these cases, scientists measure the wavelength in meters. As the frequency of a radio wave increases, the size used to measure the wavelength decreases. So in the case of a higher radio frequency (for example 2 gigahertz, or GHz), the wavelength is measured in inches or centimeters instead of feet or meters. Gigahertz is not the upper level either. Wavelengths can even be measured in smaller units such as nanometers. Depending on the wavelength, a scientist will use different devices to measure the data, including antennas, oscilloscopes, and radios.

Breaking Down Waves

FOUR

Examining the Behaviors of Waves

I t's great to understand the basics of all waves, the different categories of waves, as well as the parts of each type of wave, but the next step toward understanding waves is studying their behavior. The first question is what happens when a wave reaches the end of its medium.

Where one medium ends and another medium begins is known as the boundary. How a wave reacts when it encounters a boundary is described as the wave's boundary behavior. Imagine yourself as a wave. You are walking down the sidewalk when you bump into a freestanding door. What do you do? Essentially, you have one of three choices. You can turn around and go back the way you came, you can open the door and walk through it, or you can walk around it to get to the other side. When a wave encounters a boundary, it has the same basic choices. It can bounce off the boundary, pass through it, or skirt around it. These different reactions, or behaviors, are known as **reflection**, **refraction**, and **diffraction**.

W eather forecasters use Doppler radar to determine the velocity, or speed and direction, of a storm. Doppler radar works on the principles of the Doppler effect. The Doppler effect is a change in the frequency or wavelength of a wave as it moves relative to an observer. Weather stations emit radio signals that reflect back off clouds and other atmospheric objects. As an object gets closer, the wavelength of the sound reflecting off of it decreases. As an object moves away, the wavelength of its reflected sound increases. The rate of change allows observers to calculate speed.

Shorter wavelengths produce higher pitches, so a siren rises in pitch as the ambulance approaches and lowers in pitch after it passes by.

The Doppler effect is also present in astronomy. When light waves change frequency, their color changes. The wavelength moves to larger values if the motion of the source is away from the observer and to smaller values if the motion is toward the observer. Blue is toward the lower end of the visible spectrum, and red is toward the higher end. Therefore, if a star is moving away from Earth, the Doppler effect will result in the star having a reddish hue, also known as red shift. If a star is moving toward Earth, it will gain a bluish hue, also known as a blue shift.

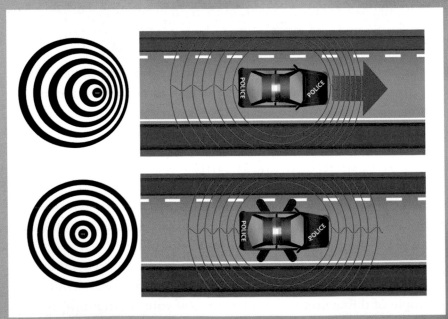

The siren's wavelength changes as a police car moves, but not when it stands still.

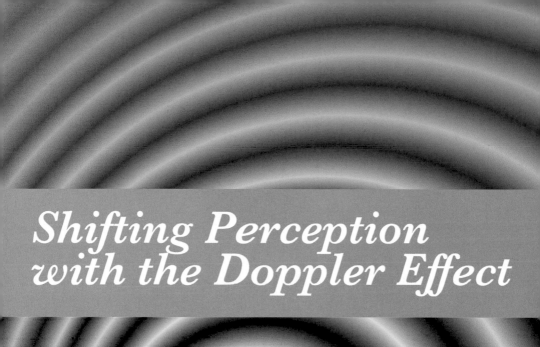

Shifting Perception with the Doppler Effect

the table, her voice is being diffracted. The wave diffracts from, or deflects from, the walls that separate the kitchen from the next room and travels to your ear.

To demonstrate diffraction in your baking dish, place two pieces of wood in the water, leaving a small gap between them. When you send a disturbance through the water with your dropper, the waves travel around the barriers.

Understanding Waves *and* Wave Motion

Feeding ducks create waves that interfere with each other.

DEALING WITH INTERFERENCE

Suppose that two separate waves meet inside the same medium. What would happen? For example, when a wave meets another wave traveling in an opposite direction in your rope, the occurrence is called interference. There are two types of interference: constructive and destructive. In constructive interference, the crests and troughs of two waves are in phase, or coincide, causing their amplitudes to increase. In a destructive interference, the crest of one wave lines up with the trough of another. When a crest is lined up with a trough, meaning that they have displacements in the opposite direction, the crest and the trough cancel each other out and the medium returns to the rest position.

A submarine uses sonar to measure its distance from other objects in the sea.

FIVE

Real-World Uses of Waves

S tudying waves and their properties is great, but seeing how the information learned can be applied in the real world makes it easier to understand why scientists want to learn as much as possible about waves. From the deepest depths of the ocean to the expansive universe, waves can help scientists learn more.

If you have ever seen a movie or read a book about submarines, you will be familiar with the term "sonar" (sound navigation ranging). Sonar is a method used by submarines and ships to navigate through the ocean or detect other submarines. When using sonar, a submarine sends out a ping (a disturbance) and waits to hear if the ping bounces back, or reflects, from a barrier. The distance between the submarine and the barrier is determined by measuring the time it takes the pulse caused by the ping to return. Using a ping to cause a wave to reflect off of a barrier, perhaps another submarine, is called active sonar. There is also another type of sonar called passive sonar. Passive sonar listens for waves without causing an initial disturbance by pinging. For example, passive sonar picks

up sound waves that are sent out by whales or other submarines using active sonar. Sonar is used on many ships to help them avoid collisions with objects below the surface of the sea.

STUDYING EARTH WITH SEISMOLOGY

Seismology is an earth science and a wave-related field. Seismologists study earthquakes, or the movement of waves through Earth's surface. By determining how seismic waves behave,

Understanding Waves and Wave Motion

The Very Large Array, a radio astronomy observatory in New Mexico, helps scientists observe radio waves from space.

seismologists have been able to discover that Earth's outer core is made of liquid. This was one of the first and most important discoveries made in seismology.

Seismologists discovered that only longitudinal waves could travel through Earth's outer core. Transverse waves cannot travel through liquid or gas. However, the waves produced by an earthquake are both transverse and longitudinal. Yet, only the longitudinal waves could travel through Earth's outer core. This discovery led scientists to conclude that Earth's outer core is made of a liquid.

STUDYING COSMIC SIGNALS

One of the newer fields in astronomy is known as radio astronomy, or the transmitting and receiving of cosmic signals. In radio astronomy, scientists measure and observe the characteristics of radio waves they receive from outer space. Since the 1930s, radio astronomy has greatly increased our knowledge of the universe. Through radio astronomy, scientists have discovered previously unknown stars and constellations, and have been able to learn more about the presence of dark matter in the universe.

Recently, a joint partnership of European, Asian, South American, and North American observatories came together to build an array of forty-five antennae in northern Chile, a number

Real-World Uses of Waves

Scientists believe that disorienting sonar is linked to the death of whales, such as this whale that washed up on a beach in the Bahamas.

Sonar and Whales

The Navy's use of sonar has attracted the attention of environmentalists concerned about its affect on marine wildlife.

Sonar systems pump out slow-moving sound waves at up to 235 dB. These waves can retain an intensity of 140 dB as far as 300 miles (480 kilometers) from their source. Sound waves of 128 dB in water are as loud as 100 dB sounds in air to humans. However, these noises still can cause whales to swim hundreds of miles (km), dive or ascend rapidly, which can cause bleeding from the eyes and ears, or to beach themselves to escape the sound.

In 2005, thirty-four whales were stranded along the Outer Banks and died during sonar training. The National Resources Defense Council has repeatedly sued to get the U.S. Navy to restrict, but not to end, its use of sonar and underwater weapons testing along the West Coast, but the U.S. Supreme Court ruled in the navy's favor. It reasoned that sonar testing was an issue of national security.

The National Marine Fisheries Service has authorized navy sonar and weapons testing off the coasts of California and Hawaii through 2018, and the navy says it will increase the frequency of its tests. In January 2014, the NRDC sued the U.S. Navy and the fisheries service under the Marine Animal Protection Act, which makes it illegal to kill or harass marine mammals.

The study of waves could help predict tsunamis, such as the one that damaged these boats in Japan in 2011.

that will gradually increase to sixty-six in 2015. This array will be used to study cold matter in some of the deepest depths of our universe.

These three examples are just some of the ways scientists and engineers have applied the knowledge gained from the study of waves. These studies have produced so many of our technological breakthroughs, helped scientists more effectively predict the day-to-day weather, and allowed us to anticipate major natural disasters, including earthquakes and tsunamis. The understanding of waves and wave motion has provided us with answers about our planet, and are leading to a deeper understanding of our universe.

Understanding Waves and Wave Motion

GLOSSARY

amplitude The distance from a crest or trough to the rest position.

compression A place in a wave in which the particles of a medium are pushed together.

crest The point of maximum upward (hill-shaped) displacement along a wave.

diffraction A behavior in which a wave travels around a barrier.

disturbance An initial displacement of energy in a medium.

elasticity A phenomenon in which energy is transported without permanently displacing matter.

electromagnetic wave A type of wave that does not require a medium to propagate.

equilibrium The rest position of a medium.

frequency The number of times a wave cycle occurs over a period of time.

longitudinal A wave characteristic in which a wave travels in a direction that is parallel to the direction of the movement of the medium.

magnitude The greatness in size or amount.

BIBLIOGRAPHY

"Basic Experiments with Ripple Tanks." Nuffieldfoundation.org. http://www.nuffieldfoundation.org/practical-physics/basic-experiments-ripple-tanks

"Categories of Waves." Physicsclassroom.com. http://www.physicsclassroom.com/Class/waves/u10l1b.cfm

"The Doppler Effect." Physicsclassroom.com. http://www.physicsclassroom.com/Class/waves/u10l3d.cfm

Elmore, William E., and Mark A. Heald. *Physics of Waves.* Mineola, NY: Dover, 1985.

Kuhn, Karl. *Basic Physics: A Self-Teaching Guide.* Wiley Self-Teaching Guides. New York, NY: Wiley, 2007.

Lewin, Walter. *For the Love of Physics: From the End of the Rainbow to the Edge of Time—A Journey Through the Wonders of Physics.* New York, NY: Simon & Schuster, 2011.

Pierce, John R. *Almost All About Waves.* Dover Books on Physics. Mineola, NY: Dover Publications, 2006.

"World's Largest Radiotelescope Completed." Presstv.com. http://presstv.com/detail/2014/06/18/367478/world-largest-radiotelescope-completed

INDEX

INDEX